The Brownie Annual

Published by special arrangement with
THE GIRL GUIDES ASSOCIATION

Edited by ROBERT MOSS

Purnell

SBN 361 04574 3
Copyright © 1979 Purnell & Sons Ltd
Published 1979 by Purnell Books, Berkshire House,
Queen Street, Maidenhead, Berkshire
Made and printed in Great Britain by
Purnell & Sons Ltd, Paulton (Bristol) and London

Here's a Brownie...

A JOLLY WORDS-AND-ACTION SONG FOR THE PACK
To be sung to the tune of
"KNICK KNACK, PADDY WHACK"

1. Here's a Brownie—gains point ONE.
   Clean nails on her fingers and thumb.
   Chorus: Knick Knack, Paddy Whack, mark it on the card.
   Here's a Brownie who's tried hard.

2. Here's a Brownie—gains point TWO.
   Lovely shine upon each shoe.
   Chorus: Knick Knack, Paddy Whack, mark it on the card.
   Here's a Brownie who's tried hard.

3. Here's a Brownie—gains point THREE.
   For she washed up after tea.
   Chorus: Knick Knack, Paddy Whack, etc.

4. Here's a Brownie—gains point FOUR.
   Smiled although her knee was sore.
   Chorus: Knick Knack, Paddy Whack, etc.

5. Here's a Brownie—gains point FIVE.
   Never last one to arrive.
   Chorus: Knick Knack, Paddy Whack, etc.

6. Here's a Brownie—gains point SIX.
   With a new girl she will mix.
   Chorus: Knick Knack, Paddy Whack, etc.

7. Here's a Brownie—gains point SEVEN.
   Carried out Challenges, ten or eleven.
   Chorus: Knick Knack, Paddy Whack, etc.

8. Here's a Brownie—gains point EIGHT.
   She skips well and stands up straight.
   Chorus: Knick Knack, Paddy Whack, etc.

9. Here's a Brownie—gains point NINE.
   Badge and belt she loves to shine.
   Chorus: Knick Knack, Paddy Whack, etc.

10. Here's a Brownie—gains point TEN.
    Helps her mother, then again!
    Chorus: Knick Knack, Paddy Whack, etc.

Hand Motions in Chorus

On KNICK
Clap left knee with right hand
On KNACK
Clap right knee with left hand
On PADDY
Clap right elbow with left hand
On WHACK
Clap left elbow with right hand

On MARK IT ON
Clap left hand to left knee and right hand to right knee
On THE CARD
Clap hands together
On HERE'S A BROWNIE WHO'S TRIED HARD
Clap left shoulder of neighbour on right, with right hand, about 7 times.

Questions

If you answer correctly fifteen out of these twenty questions you have done well.

1—When is Thinking Day?

2—What Brownie Interest Badge has an arrow on it?

3—When you cross a road you should first do the three things. What are they?

4—What compass point is opposite to south-west?

5—What do three upright fingers in the Brownie salute remind you of?

6—What colours appear on St. Andrew's flag?

7—What are Brownie Revels?

8—At what age can you join Guides?

9—What must water do before tea can be made with it?

10—What other Sixes could there be in a Brownie Pack besides Pixies, Gnomes, Sprites and Elves?

11—What are the names of the two children in the *Story of the Brownies*?

12—When is St. George's Day?

13—What is the sign for "R" in semaphore and in the Morse code?

14—What does the Country Code tell you to do with gates in the country?

15—When is St. Andrew's Day?

16—When is St. David's Day?

17—In what country is a Brownie called a Kabouter?

18—What were Brownies first called?

19—Which knot is used to join two ropes of equal thickness?

20—Where on your uniform would you wear the World Badge?

The Sunflower Venture

by Dorothy Richardson

Sandra poked her head out of her bedroom window and took a deep breath of summer morning air. Down below in the garden she could see her sunflower with its beautiful velvety brown centre and huge golden petals. It had reached the top of the fence between the gardens already.

The Brownies were all growing sunflowers for a special Venture to raise money for a local charity. Their parents and friends had each agreed to pay them a certain number of pennies for every thirty centimetres the sunflowers grew. Sandra had already been promised two pounds altogether, and if her flower kept on growing there would be more to come.

From her place at the window she could see part of the next-door garden. She sighed and thought of her best friend, Joanna, who had lived there up to last month. She and Joanna had been in the same Pack and in the same form at school. Every afternoon they would play in each other's garden, creeping through the secret hole in the fence. But since Joanna and her family had moved away, the hole had been blocked up; an old lady and her daughter had come to live next door.

Sandra had caught a glimpse of the lady, Mrs Harrison, once or twice. She had white hair and glasses, and looked severe. Sandra had already decided she didn't like her, and though Mum said Mrs Harrison's daughter, who was out at work all day, was very nice and seemed friendly Sandra decided she didn't want anything to do with them. It wasn't fair that people like that should come in place of her friend and her happy-go-lucky family.

In the Brownie hall there was a chart on the wall with the names of all the Brownies who were growing sunflowers, and the height of each flower was marked up at every Pack meeting. Before setting off for the meeting that evening Sandra would measure the sunflower again; she was almost sure that hers was the tallest. The Pixie Sixer, Mary, had grown a sunflower only five centimetres shorter than hers, and Sandra hoped to have the tallest one in the whole Pack.

"I'm just going down to the shops," her mother said soon after Sandra returned from school that afternoon. "I won't be long, but you'll probably be gone to Brownies before I get back. Don't be late. I've left your subscription money on the hall table."

"All right, Mum; I'm going to get ready now." Sandra ran upstairs to her bedroom and changed into her uniform.

It was only after the hall-door closed that she remembered she had forgotten to ask for a tape-measure to measure the sunflower. She took a quick look through her mother's workbasket, but there was no tape there. Out in the garden the sunflower was stirring gently in the breeze.

Sandra went out and gazed up at the golden head.

"If I was up there I might be able to guess how high I was from the ground," she thought.

She fetched the household steps, which were kept in the kitchen, and carried them into the garden, placing them beside the sunflower. When she stood on the top step her head was a

The sunflower was up to the top of the fence

little higher than the petals.

"Hello! I've been admiring your sunflower. I'm glad it's grown tall enough to look at us over the fence," said a soft voice.

Sandra started and found herself staring at Mrs Harrison, who was sitting on a seat in the next-door garden, knitting.

"Your daddy must be a very good gardener to grow a plant so tall, and with such a fine bloom," said Mrs Harrison.

"I—I grew it myself," Sandra told the old lady. "It's a special sunflower for Brownies, but I don't know how tall it is because I can't find the tape-measure and Mum is out." She hadn't meant to say all that, but somehow it just came out.

"Oh, perhaps I can help you; I have one in the house. Would you like to come round to the hall door and I'll get it for you?"

Sandra was just about to say, "It doesn't matter," but it would at least be a chance to find out the real height of the flower, so she climbed down from the ladder and made her way to the front door of the next house.

The door was already open, and Mrs Harrison was standing there. Sandra noticed she had twinkly blue eyes behind her glasses. She was smiling. She didn't look at all cross.

"Come in!"

Sandra followed the old lady across the hall and into the living-room, where the french doors opened on to the garden.

"Oh!" She stared around her in surprise. It all looked very different from when Joanna lived there. The walls had been freshly papered with a pretty golden-coloured paper, and the armchairs were brown with bright orange-and-gold cushions. There were pictures on the walls, and Sandra looked at them as Mrs Harrison opened a polished wooden workbasket. The tape was soon found.

In the corner of the room, set on a high shelf, was a huge vase, painted in soft, glowing colours, and in it stood some bronze-coloured dried leaves and tall grasses.

"What a pretty vase!" said Sandra.

"Yes, isn't it," agreed Mrs Harrison, "I've had it for many years and I'm very fond of it; the colours go so well with this room. I dried some beech-leaves last year, and they've lasted all this time. I brought them with me when we moved. Here is the tape-measure." She handed it to Sandra. "Won't it be difficult to measure it by yourself? I think I had better come and hold it at the bottom while you climb up the steps."

"Thank you," said Sandra. Mrs Harrison was turning out to be quite a different sort of person from her first idea of her.

Back in her own garden, Sandra climbed the steps again.

"What a pretty vase!" said Sandra, looking at a vase in the corner

Mrs Harrison held the tape at the base of the sunflower.

"A hundred and eighty-eight centimetres!" Sandra exclaimed, nearly falling off the steps in her excitement. "Mine will probably be the tallest!" She told Mrs Harrison all about the sunflower Venture. "I must go now," she ended, as the clock indoors struck half-past four.

"Let me know if yours was the tallest, won't you?" said Mrs Harrison, and Sandra promised.

"Why, it's a dead-heat for Mary and Sandra!" exclaimed the Brownie Guider as she chalked up the heights on the wall-chart at Pack meeting. "Only one more week to go and then we'll collect the money, so you'll all have a chance that your flowers will grow a tiny bit more."

That evening before going to bed Sandra gave the sunflower a good watering. There hadn't been any rain for a long time, and the garden looked very dry.

"Grow, grow, just a few more centimetres, please!" she begged, looking up at the golden petals.

But that night disaster struck. Who would have believed it? Snug in bed, Sandra awoke to hear torrents of rain beating against the window and the wind howling in the chimney. There was a flash of lightning and a crash of thunder. She buried her head under the clothes and tried not to listen. When the noise finally died away she fell asleep again.

In the morning it was still windy, but the rain had stopped and the sun was shining. Sandra ran to the window. How fresh and green everything seemed after the rain! Leaves were strewn on the grass and the

The sunflower lay flat, its stem broken

flowers were—"Oh!" Sandra shrieked in horror and stared. Her sunflower! Her beautiful flower had been battered by the wind and lay flat across the flower-bed, its stem broken! She ran downstairs in her pyjamas, and out into the garden. The stem was cracked right across, about halfway from the flower. She lifted it up and burst into tears.

"Don't cry, darling," comforted her father, coming out into the garden. "Look at my roses. Every bloom is destroyed! These things do happen to gardeners from time to time, and we've just got to be brave and take the disappointments. Look!" He took a garden-knife. "We'll cut the stem right off where it's broken, and you can take the flower indoors and put it in a vase."

Sandra choked back her sobs and carried the sunflower into the house. When the wet earth was wiped off the petals the bloom was still nearly perfect.

"I haven't a vase tall enough to take that long stem," said her mother, after searching the kitchen cupboard, "and if we cut the stem shorter it won't look right with that huge head."

"I'd like to take it to Brownies next week to show Brown Owl and the others what it was like," Sandra said, "so I'll put it in a bucket of water and keep it until then."

"Yes, that's a good idea," agreed her mother, and she took out a plastic bucket from under the sink to put the sunflower in.

But later that morning a sudden idea occurred to Sandra. The idea seemed better and better the more she thought about it. Suddenly she decided not to waste any time. Taking the sunflower from the bucket, she hurried

8

"I'm just doing a crayon drawing of the vase and the leaves," she explained. "I like painting and drawing, and I was wishing I had a flower to put amongst the leaves to give the picture more colour. Then you rang the bell, and my wish was granted! When the flower is finished, I'll collect the seeds and we'll both plant some next year and see how we get on. Would you like that?"

Sandra nodded happily.

"Now," said Mrs Harrison, "I should like to give you something." She opened a drawer. "I like to take photographs. Your mother allowed me into your garden, and I took a colour picture of your sunflower. Here it is. It will show your Brownie Guider what a very fine flower you grew before the storm cut it off."

Sandra gazed with delight at the colour print Mrs Harrison handed to her. The sun had caught the sunflower in its light, and the flower stood out tall and straight and beautiful.

"Oh, thank you!" cried Sandra. "Why, it's almost as good as having the real sunflower, and I shall be able to show it to everybody and keep it. I shall put it up on my wall."

When she next set off for Pack meeting, Sandra's smile was as sunny as the sunflower's. In her pocket was the lovely picture, which Daddy had promised to make a frame for, and now Brown Owl and the Brownies would really be able to see what a lovely sunflower she had grown.

"It's perfect!" exclaimed Mrs Harrison

round to Mrs Harrison's front door and rang the bell.

Mrs Harrison's eyes opened wide in surprise when she saw Sandra standing there, holding the sunflower. Sandra held it out.

"It broke off in the wind last night," she explained. "We've got nowhere to put it and I thought it would fit in that lovely vase in your sitting-room. I'd like you to have it."

"Oh, what a shame it was damaged!" Mrs Harrison took the flower. "It must be a great disappointment for you. Yes, I would love to have it. Come in and we'll see how it looks. It was kind of you to think of me."

In the sitting-room she placed the sunflower amongst the leaves and the golden grasses. The stem was exactly the right length for the vase.

"It's perfect!" Mrs Harrison exclaimed. She pointed to a large sheet of paper and some crayons and pencils strewn on the sofa.

HOW TO MAKE

Jelly Dishes

Here's a new way with jellies. Cut round margarine containers to about 6.5cm (2½") high and set jellies in them. Two chocolate drops for eyes and a jelly bean for a mouth will give them faces.

Before pouring the jelly into containers to set, rinse the containers first in cold water. Do not dry, as the moistness will help the jelly to slide out easily when you run a knife round the edge. You may, of course, prefer to leave the jellies in the containers instead of turning them out on to plates.

The tops of soft-margarine containers make suitable plates, especially the plastic type. For a pretty effect you could add thick cream or custard round your jelly. It makes your mouth water, doesn't it?

DO-IT-YOURSELF

Decorations

For Christmas or party decorations, paint pine or fir cones with silver paint. Tie gay tinsel cord round the pointed ends, and fasten to another length of tinsel or tinsel cord. Hung from bough to bough and shining in the light, they look lovely.

Silver Chains: Save all the milk-bottle caps you can. Wash them clean. With scissors, make a cut in the centre of each cap and then tear the metal back. Now wrap the middle parts round the outside part; this will make a ring. Make two like this. Begin another one, but before rolling the ends up cut the rim and join the other two rings. Then, with the two cut ends overlapping, wrap the inside of the middle ring as before. Now you have three rings. So you can go on. The more caps you have the longer your chain. You need only cut open half the rings, of course. Some caps are of red metal-foil, and these would make your chain more colourful.

Pint~size Ponies

Bandphotos

Left:
Debbie goes for a walk with her Tom Thumb ponies, who are the same size as her dog

Below:
"Gee up!" says Lee, who is off for a drive with his mini gipsy caravan, drawn by a mini horse

Meet the world's smallest horses. They are the pets of Debbie and Lee Andrew, who live in Exeter. They are only 62cm (2 ft.) high and weigh less than 36 lbs. They wander about the Andrew house, trot up and down stairs, and relax on the sofa. They make you want to cuddle them, don't they?

FIND THE OWL
says Daphne M. Pilcher

Who finds the owl—the Elf or the Sprite?

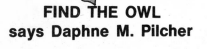

Brownie

HA, HA, HA!

What did the big chimney say to the little chimney?
You're too young to smoke.

There were two flies on a door. Which was the angry one?
The one that flew off the handle.

Why does a sick pig never get well?
Because he has to be killed before he's cured.

Don't tell your troubles to an owl;
You may as well stay mute;
For any troubles save his own
He doesn't give a hoot.

LOLLIE DOLLIES
Margaret Law Tells You How to Make Them

For the Brownie stall at a church bazaar, my Brownies made lollie dollies. They were delightful, easy to make, quick to sell. To make them you need: lollipops, drinking straws, circular tissue paper approx. 12.7cm (5 ins.) in diameter, cotton, yellow gummed paper cut into the shape of faces, and cellophane paper.

Now here's how to make them:

Cover lollipop with cellophane paper and stick a yellow face on either side. Make a hole through the centre of the straw and push the stick of the lollipop through the hole. Make a hole through the centre of the tissue paper and push the stick through it. Bend paper down to form blouse part of dress and tie cotton round the waist. Cut the straws to the correct size and draw in the face. Your lollie dolly should look like the one illustrated, only better, because yours will have a yellow face and a coloured dress.

Bran Tub

WHAT DO BROWNIES DO?
A Poem by *Morag Leslie*, a Guide of the 138th A Edinburgh Company

Brownies are helpful,
And good to have around.
In the early morning
They work without a sound.

When the rain is pouring down,
And the sun has gone away,
They brighten us all up—
They are cheerful all the day.

Polishing the table,
Singing as they go,
Doing chores around the house,
Help us when we feel low.

When I'm old and grey
Won't it be nice to know
They will work and cheer me up
Singing as they go!

THE LAND OF NOD
by Aileen E. Passmore

The Land of Nod is beyond the moon
And across the silvery sea;
It's turn to the right and turn to the left
And over the tallest tree.
It's a wonderful land, is the Land of Nod,
With fields of woolly white sheep,
But no-one is ever allowed in there,
Unless they are fast asleep!

DIAL A LETTER

Can you discover the missing letter on the telephone dial? You won't find it on a real telephone, which has numbers only.

SNAIL MAIL

A Gloucestershire Brownie recently received a birthday card through the post with a big hole in the middle. The postman apologised for it. "A snail's been at it," he explained. "It sometimes happens in rural districts. The snails crawl into the post-boxes from the hedges, and they spend the night chewing at letters."

SQUIRREL PUZZLE

Take away a letter from each word, then join together what is left to make an animal found in the British Isles.

1—Tot Bad, 2—Ham Red, 3—Mob Let, 4—Set Pal, 5—Stop Ate, 6—Mop Used, 7—Crab Bite, 8—Squire Reel.

Mary's Countryside Flowers

by Philip J. Randall

Lady's Smock

"What is that on your finger?" Michelle asked Tracy, her Sixer.

"A ladybird," Tracy answered, and she recited:

"Ladybird, ladybird, fly away home;
Your house is on fire, your children all gone:
All except one, and that's little Ann,
And she has crept under the warming-pan."

Then, very gently, Tracy blew on the gaily-coloured little beetle. Its bright-red, black-spotted wingcase parted and the insect flew away.

"She's gone!" Michelle cried.

Every Brownie knows the rhyme, but not even many grown-ups know the proper meaning of the words. You see, the rhyme is so old that its origin has been completely forgotten. One mistake Michelle made was to call the ladybird "she". There are "he's" as well. The name has nothing to do with the insect being male or female, but was given long ago at a time when the people of England paid extra special respect to Mary the mother of Jesus. They called her "Our Lady"; some do so still. So it came about that the pretty spotted beetle was called "Our Lady's Bird", now shortened to Ladybird.

Round about the same period some wildflowers were named

Lady's Fingers

Lady's Tresses

Lady's Mantle

Lady's Bedstraw

after Mary. You might look for some of them next time the Pack has an outing in the country.

LADY'S SMOCK is easy to find in riverside meadows in spring. Because of the gentle fragrance of this pale-mauve flower, children in some parts call it "Smell Smock". Another name is "Cuckoo Flower".

LADY'S FINGERS is common in early summer where the soil is chalky. The cluster of deep-yellow flowers, sometimes tipped with red, could be said to look like fingers, although some children think they are shaped like tiny rashers of bacon and call the plant "Eggs and Bacon". Another name is "Kidney Vetch".

LADY'S BEDSTRAW flowers in hedgerows and on banks all through the summer. The clusters of yellow flowers might be said to be like tiny lilac blooms.

Less common are *LADY'S MANTLE*, which produces a very small greenish-yellow flower in spring and summer, and *LADY'S TRESSES*, the flowers of which are white and sweetly scented. It is found during the summer in northern England on bogland. This is also known as "Creeping Lady's Tresses". There is an autumn variety found on downland.

**"Ladybird, ladybird, fly away home!"
chanted Tracy**

Play 'Brownie Badges'

Jean Howard Tells You How

This game can be played indoors or out of doors. Pack Leader can supervise it while your Guider is doing something else.

Pack Leader makes a set of cards, each with a different Interest Badge on it. Could Pack Leader draw them and the Brownies colour them?

Start with twelve cards. This number could be increased as you become good at the game.

The Sixes sit in groups fairly near together. Pack Leader deals each Six three cards (or four if there are only three Sixes). Don't let the other Sixes see or hear what you have got. Each Six also has a list of all the badges in the pack.

Pack Leader tells one Six to start. The Sixer asks one of the other Sixes for, say, Cyclist. If the Six have it they must pass it over. If not they will say "Sorry —not at home." Then it is their turn to ask a Six for a card on the list. Each Six must listen carefully so that when it is their turn they will remember where the various badges are. The Six to get possession of all the cards is the winner.

When you have had several games, try playing without the list of badges; this will be a good memory test.

Our Pack Holiday

by Catherine Laffeaty

On Friday evening we took our luggage to the church hall, so that we didn't have to carry it all down the next morning.

When Saturday arrived, I got up early and had breakfast. Then Mummy, my two sisters and my brother came down to the Church Hall to see me off. The coach was already there and quite a lot of Brownies and their parents were outside the hall. When all the Brownies had arrived we got into the coach with Brown Owl and Tawny Owl, and the driver started up the engine. The mums and dads started waving, and we were off.

Soon we were out in the country, and some of the Brownies in the back of the coach started singing songs they had learnt at school. The sun was shining and it made the coach very hot, so the driver opened the window in the

roof to cool us off. On the way, we stopped outside a farm and had a run round. After that, we took off our belts because the driver thought we would feel

Elevenses for the Stoats

much better without them.

When we arrived, the other Guiders and Pack Leaders were already at the hall we had borrowed at Middleton-on-Sea. It was in a private road next to St. Nicholas' Church. We took our belongings inside and put up our camp beds. Then we got into our three Sixes, the Stoats, Weasels and Ferrets. I was a Stoat.

We had different jobs every day. First I was a waitress and we had to lay the table for dinner. After dinner we took the cutlery and dishes and glasses outside and washed them. Then it was rest hour and we took groundsheets outside and then sat and read books or comics and wrote

Rise and shine, wash faces, and brush hair—first morning on Pack holiday

An easy way to climb a tree—or is it? ▼

Many hands make light work of washing up ▲

letters or postcards home.

Later in the afternoon we went down to the beach. We were allowed to paddle, but one or two Brownies fell in the water and had to change their clothes.

The next day was Sunday, so we went to church in the morning and in the afternoon to the beach. Some of the Brownies had a sand-castle competition. That night some of the Brownies had to have a bath, but I didn't want one, so I ran away, but I had to have one the next night.

On Tuesday it was Deborah's birthday, and we went to the Pets' Corner at Bognor Zoo. Then we went to a boating pond and we all had a ride. After this we had a party tea.

The next day our Division Commissioner came, and we all waved streamers that we had made from coloured crepe paper. In the afternoon, we went to the beach with Commissioner, and she dipped her toes into the sea!

Another day we had a treasure hunt. Brown Owl had borrowed a field and the Pack Leaders had cut out paper arrows for us to follow. The group I was in found the treasure first, but it was only an empty box. However, a note in the box said we had to go to Brown Owl, so we did. Brown Owl had the treasure and we all got some sweets.

Friday was the day we went home. But in the morning we went to the beach and had another sand-castle competition. I came third and I got some sweets, but all the losers had some sweets as well. We had a picnic dinner outside the hall, but the coach arrived early without the key to the back of the coach where we were to put our luggage, so the Guiders had to break the lock (it was an old

coach) while we finished our dinner. Then we loaded our luggage and ourselves and said goodbye to the other Guiders, who were going to follow us in the car after they had locked up the hall. On the way we stopped, and Brown Owl gave us some cake and milk and we saw the other Guiders overtake us.

When we were nearly home we sang, "For He's a Jolly Good Fellow" to the driver, but he

didn't take much notice. We got to the Church Hall just after the Guiders, who were busy talking to our parents. I said thank you to Brown Owl for taking me on such a lovely holiday. Then I went home, feeling very sad to be back again; but there is always next year.

Exciting discoveries on the seashore before leaving for home

Photos: Miss W. J. Beer

Puzzle Pie

by Daphne M. Pilcher

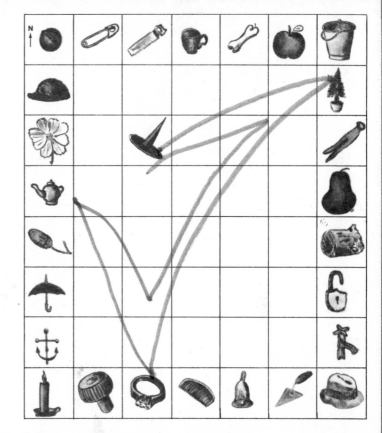

WHAT HAS THE WITCH BECOME?

Witches, of course, can change into almost anything. All this one has left behind is her hat. Starting at the hat, follow the compass directions and see what the witch becomes. 2E, 3S, 1W, 1NE, 1NW, 1SW, 2E, 2NW, 3S, 3NE, 1E.

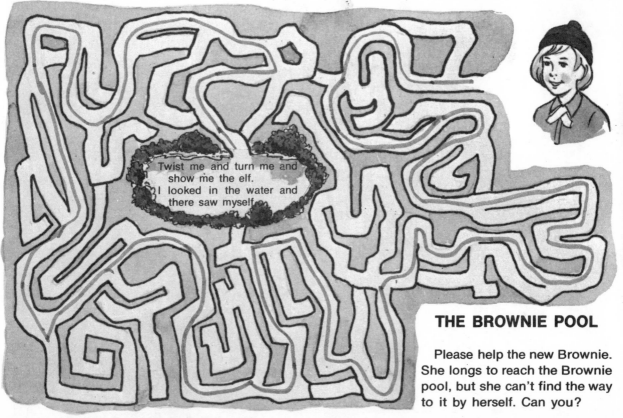

Twist me and turn me and show me the elf.
I looked in the water and there saw myself.

THE BROWNIE POOL

Please help the new Brownie. She longs to reach the Brownie pool, but she can't find the way to it by herself. Can you?

Flags and Pennants

Abigail Gwyther carries the 1st Roch Pack's pennant to a "Blessing of the Flags" ceremony at St. Mary's Church, Roch, Pembrokeshire (1)

Colour print by Mrs J. A. Gwyther

This caterpillar's got Brownie legs. They belong to the 12th Loughborough Pack, who made it and won first prize with it in the Shelthorpe Gala (3)

Colour print by Miss A. Hallam

The 24th Colchester Pack proudly carry the banner, made by themselves, with which they won the Brownie trophy (2)

Colour print by Mrs O. Sheppard

Karen Streather cleans the Pack pennant in readiness for a church parade by the 1st Pilgrim's Hatch Brownies, Essex (4)

Colour print by Mrs M. R. Hills

The Promise ceremony, in which the new Brownie makes her Promise and receives her badge (1)

"I looked in the water and there saw myself" (2)

The owl likes to sit on the toadstool in the Brownie Ring and look and listen (3)

This is the Brownie salute, which — don't forget!—is always done with a smile (4)

The New Brownie

Colour prints by Mrs B. M. Hall and Mrs E. Rothwell

HOW TO MAKE

MAKE YOUR OWN

Necklace

Lena Baker Tells You How

Make an attractive, bead-like necklace for wearing with your best dress.

You will need a length of white or cream-coloured cotton, a needle, a fastener (which can be bought at a handicraft shop for a few pence), and beech-nuts.

What you do is thread your needle with a long length of cotton and tie a knot at the end.

Next separate the beech-nuts from the bristly husks—they usually fall out easily. Now thread them on to the cotton. You will find that they fall together so that no cotton shows. Continue until you have your necklace the right length, then fix on your fastener, one piece to each end of the cotton.

This necklace will last a very long time, and it has a nice, woody, varnished appearance. If you prefer, you could paint the beech-nuts a gay colour before threading them on to the cotton.

Leave It to You
by Ruth Hoult

Here is a fun way to make different shapes into animals, objects, or even people. All you need to begin is some leaves.

Place the leaves on a piece of paper and draw round them. Then look at the shapes you have. If you use your imagination you will be able to draw all sorts of things. Here are some leaf shapes to help you begin.

Poplar leaf: This is an easy shape; it makes a teapot. All you need to do is add the handle, lid and spout.

Willow leaf: From this you can make a lovely, long fish. All you have to do is draw in the fins, tail and head. Don't forget the scales to make it look realistic.

Sycamore leaf: This is a more difficult shape. But it makes a person skipping, or without the rope a ballerina. Draw in the face and hands and legs and feet, then the line to make the skirt. Add the rope if you want to.

Alder leaf: This is a good face shape. It can make the cat, as shown, or a mouse, and it makes a human face, too. It is good fun to try the different ones.

Beech leaf: This is a good one to draw; it makes so many things: first a mouse, just by adding a tail, nose, whiskers, and eye. See how easy it makes a ladybird, too. It will also make a different shape of fish. If you draw two side by side, add a body and a head, you have a butterfly.

It's fun, isn't it, and it will help you to tell which leaves belong to different trees.

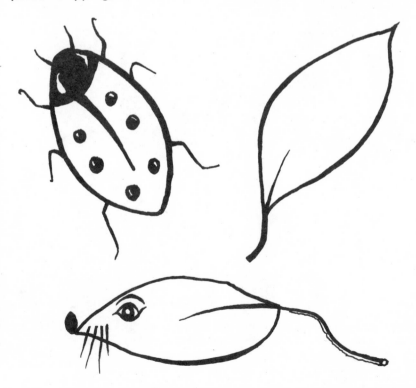

Emily's Doll's House

Emily Kramer's doll's house cost eight hundred pounds—and it's worth every penny.

It has eight rooms, all fully furnished, with expensive wallpaper and wall-to-wall carpets. All the furnishings are hand-made in antique style. Doors have proper hinges, and the drawers of tables, cabinets and chests open just like those of full-size furniture.

Some of the pieces cost as much as forty pounds each.

Emily's beautiful doll's house is one of many made by Peter and Michael Hunt in Sudbury, Suffolk, who design each house themselves.

You may not be able to afford a doll's house of this quality, but perhaps you'll get some useful ideas for your own by looking at the interior of Emily's.

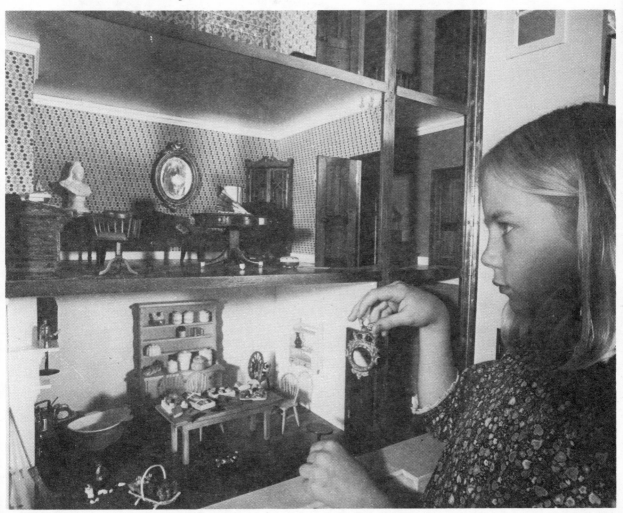

Happy Days

Story time with Tawny Owl for some of the 46th Bolton (Blackrod Methodist) Pack on Pack Holiday at Harrogate (1)

Colour slide by Mrs M. Taylor

Swing high, swing low—a happy holiday snap of Brownies of the 6th Beeston (St. Mary's) Pack, Leeds (2)

Colour slide by Miss S. J. Owen

This Brownie from the 5th Camberley Pack on Pack Holiday at Beaverbrook Lodge can hardly walk for laughing and decides she's not cut out for tight-rope walking (3)

Colour slide by Mrs A. L. Westcott

Looking at their scrap-books passes a happy hour indoors for Brownies of the Chryston District of North Lanarkshire, Scotland (4)

Colour slide by Miss E. Paterson

Michelle is not only working for the Animal Lover Badge—she's enjoying it! Michelle belongs to the 1st Tunbridge Wells (St. Luke's) Pack (5)

Colour slide by Miss Daphne M. Pilcher

3

5

Peter and the Snowman

Written for the Writer Badge by Victoria Hewitt, of the 10th Bournemouth (St Katharine's) Pack

One winter day Peter woke up feeling very cold. He got out of bed. He went to the window and looked out. He saw lots of snow on the ground. "Oh good!" he said and quickly got dressed and ran downstairs. He put on a hat and coat, got the key and opened the door. He saw lots more snow than before, about half a foot deep. He quietly ran outside and started to build a snowman. He rolled a little snowball all round the garden until it was very big, then rolled it into the middle of the garden. He made a smaller one for the head, with two buttons for eyes and a stone for the nose. Peter found a stick for his mouth and an old scarf. Then he saw a light in his mother's and father's bedroom, so quickly he ran inside, took off his hat and coat and laid the table for breakfast. After breakfast he went outside and suddenly someone called to him. "Peter!" the voice called, so Peter ran inside and asked his mother, "Did you call me?"

"No," said his mother. "You must have imagined it."

Peter asked his father, "Did you call me?"

"No," said his father. "Perhaps it was the snowman."

So Peter went outside to see if it was the snowman, and to his surprise he saw the snowman waving his arms in the air and calling "Peter! Peter!" at the top of his voice.

Just then his mother called, "Peter, come in for dinner."

Peter had dinner and was just about to go outside when Mother said, "We are going to see Auntie Anne today; come and get ready to go."

When they came home it was time to go to bed. So he got undressed. After his mother and father had gone to bed, he woke up because he heard a noise coming from the garden. He got up and got dressed. He ran downstairs, got the key and opened the door. The snowman had been calling to him. Peter found his torch and switched it on. The snowman said, "Go inside and get some food to eat."

When Peter came back with some food and drink the snowman told Peter that they were going to Snowland.

Peter asked, "How are we going to get there?"

The snowman said, "We shall fly there."

"But how?" said Peter. "We have not got an aeroplane."

"I know," said the snowman. "I can fly. Hold on to me and I will take you to Snowland."

The snowman said some magic words and soon they were flying above the clouds. Suddenly they landed on the ground with a bump. Peter saw lots of snowmen. Some of them looked like children and others like grown-ups and animals. Then the snowman took Peter to see the King of Snowmen. The King was called Andrew, and the snowman was called John. The King said that Peter could go all round Snowland to see every-

thing. Then John took Peter to his house to have something to eat. But then Peter said, "If you live here, how did I make you?"

"I am magic, as you know," said John. "I was made up in snow by you, but I broke myself up so you could make me again."

"That was clever," said Peter, not quite understanding what he meant.

"Come on in," said John. "I will make a fire."

Soon Peter and John were sitting chatting and sipping hot coffee when suddenly someone knocked at the door.

"Come in," said John.

In came a little boy.

"Sit down," said John.

The little boy sat down. "The giant is coming!" he said.

"The giant!" said Peter.

"Yes," said John. "Here he comes now. Hurry into the kitchen."

"It is very cold in here," said Peter.

"Sh!" said the snowman. "He is just outside."

"Help! The house is falling down on me!" said Peter.

"Dig yourself out quickly," said John. "The giant has gone now."

They built the house again. When it was finished it was time for Peter to go home.

"Stand in this circle," said John.

He said some magic words and Peter found himself back in his garden. He went inside, took off his hat and coat and laid the table for breakfast.

HOW TO MAKE
by Lena Baker

Bird Titbits

Birds can make use of most household meal-scraps. A nylon fruit-bag, the kind supermarkets pack fruit in, is good for stuffing scraps into and for hanging up outside.

Almost any scraps will do: left-over boiled rice, stale cake, minced beef, bacon rind, scraps of cheese, etc.

Another way to feed the birds in winter at no cost to yourself is to collect berries and nuts for them during the autumn. Pick the berries when they are just ripe. Conkers, chestnuts, acorns and beech-mast are best collected as soon as they have fallen. Dry the berries in a warm airing cupboard, and store both these and the nuts in a dry, dark place.

Birds love peanuts, and many species like fruit, cut up. Old apples, oranges, bananas and tomatoes are all welcomed. Don't worry that you may be offering the wrong things; birds will usually leave alone anything that doesn't suit them.

Birds of the acrobatic tit family love boiled and crushed chestnuts. Acorns, hazel-nuts and beech-nuts should be grated or chopped before being offered to your feathered friends.

For an extra treat, pour fat over the scraps you put out, but do make sure that your bird feeding spot is out of the reach of cats. Remember too that birds need water in winter when their usual drinking-supply may be frozen up.

Bird Pudding

Make your bird friends this pudding for Christmas. They would enjoy it at any time of the year, but there are usually more scraps left over at Christmas.

Seeds, old cake, bits of cheese, oatmeal, Christmas pudding remains, and turkey scraps are all acceptable. You need about half a pound of melted fat as well, an empty plastic-type margarine container or yogurt container, and a length of string.

What You Do. First make a hole in the bottom of the margarine container. Thread the string through this and tie a knot.

Mix all your scraps together in a bowl and stuff these into the margarine container.

Warm the fat until it is runny, then carefully pour it over the scraps and allow to set. All you have to do then is hang your pudding in the garden and watch the birds enjoy it. As sparrows cannot easily get at it, you may like to scatter some scraps around for them as well, where a cat isn't likely to surprise them.

Brownies of the 4th Christchurch Pack put a smile on a car during a "Lend a Hand" project

Colour print by Miss G. Aslett

Nature study for these Lancashire lasses begins with looking at leaves and identifying the trees on which they grow. The Brownies belong to the 5th Aughton (St. Michael) Pack, near Ormskirk

Colour print by Mrs E. Rothwell

Chocolate eggs to give to elderly folk is the unusual Easter Pack Venture these Brownies of the 1st Badingham Pack are engaged in—and not one of them is dipping a finger in the tempting mixture to taste it!

Colour print by Mrs P. J. Oakley

Lending a Hand

All the Brownies of the 9th High Barnet Salvation Army Pack joined in making this fine knitted blanket for a children's home overseas

Colour print by Mrs J. M. Chester

Home and Abroad

The 1st Bures Brownies made paper flowers and dressed up as flowers in a garden for their float in the local carnival (1)

Colour print by Mrs S. Kempson

Brownie Scouts take part in the ceremony of raising the flag at camp in Ueda, Japan (2)

Colour print by Mrs K. P. Morey

Here comes the bride, who is the Brownie Guider of the 1st Starbeck Pack, Yorkshire, and who was greeted by a guard of honour of her Brownies (3)

Colour print by Mrs B. Warren

These are the twenty-five-pound St. Issell's Brownies, "Red Crow and Tribe", who won the first prize of £25 and a silver cup in the Saundersfoot carnival, Pembrokeshire (4)

Colour print by Mrs M. McDowall

29

Tricky Teasers

by G. R. Siddons

COUNT THE CUBES
How many cubes are there?

HONEYCOMB MAZE
Can you guide the bee out of the honeycomb?

COLOUR THE CLOWNS
Can you find one difference in the two clowns? When you've done so, colour both of them.

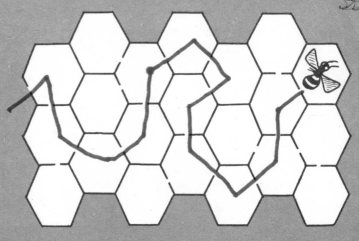

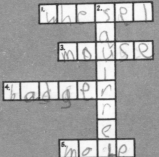

OUTLINE CROSSWORD
What are the animals outlined? If you guess correctly, their names will fit into the squares—1, 3, 4 and 5 across and 2 down.

Our Brownie Revels

by M. Atkins

Brownie Revels are always great fun. They take various forms. Our Brownies —about a hundred from the East Grinstead area of Sussex—were castaways on a desert island. All the Guiders and Pack Leaders were dressed as pirates, and the Brownies as castaways. There were ten different teams, and they were named after famous pirates or buccaneers like Kidd, Morgan, Avery, Teach, and Drake.

During the afternoon each team had to complete ten different challenges. Remember, we were all on a desert island, so a lot of imagination had to be used for some of the challenges. Nothing much grew on this island except coconuts, so we had to knock these out of the tree to get something to eat. Our tree was a netball post, so each time a

goal was scored that was one coconut off the tree.

Some kind of shelter was needed, and this had to be built from cloth and wood salvaged from the boat. There was a stream through the middle of the island, and the only way to get across it was to swing over, using a rope slung from a tree. The whole afternoon was full of exciting happenings, like walking the plank. Driftwood had to be collected so that a fire could be made.

There was hidden treasure on the island, guarded by the pirates, and only one way to find it. After each challenge was completed, every Brownie received a part of a map. When all ten pieces of the map were placed together it showed where the treasure was. Then everyone raced for the treasure chest.

Everyone needed a rest after all the noise and excitement, so the Brownies ate their picnic tea and the Guiders added up the points awarded to each team for their challenges to find the winners.

Our Brownie Revels ended with a lovely singsong. We all joined in the many songs we knew and learned new ones.

Revels, parties and plays give Brownies a good opportunity to dress up, which they love to do. These horrifying witches with masks and tall hats and claw-like hands are really Brownies of the 24th Colchester Pack enjoying their Hallowe'en Party

Photo by courtesy of the Essex County Standard

The little dogs made by the 9th and 12th Loughborough Brownies on Pack Holiday don't bark; but they are gifts the mums will love

The Loughborough Brownies made all kinds of things to dress up in at their Easter fancy-dress party

Brownies Make Things

Mummy is going to love the Christmas gift Clare Waterfield is decorating with seashells

These Brownies are making too—making their badges shine

Colour prints by Miss A. Hallam

Katie's Kinkajou

This curious creature is a kinkajou, and is the unusual pet of Katie Smith, of Exmouth. Kinkajous live in the rain-forests of South America, but this furry baby is quite at home hanging upside-down in Katie's bedroom and likes to share his mistress's bedtime story

Bandphotos

"I can read it better this way"

"I can't see properly from here"

The Surprise Picnic

by Mervyn Manson

"**I'm fed up**," said Mandy Adams, kicking at her slipper, which had fallen off and which narrowly missed the clock as it flew through the air.

"So am I," agreed Susan, her sister, who was sprawled on the settee in front of the fire. "There's absolutely nothing to do."

It was a bright but cold February day, and the girls were on half-term holiday. They had got up that morning about ten o'clock, done some shopping for their Aunt Janet, and for the last hour had mooned about with nothing to do.

"What's the matter now?" said Aunt Janet, coming in at that moment with a bucket of coal. She was a young aunt, with whom they were staying whilst their parents were abroad.

"We've nothing to do," Mandy told her.

"We're bored," added Susan.

"Bored? How can you be bored? There are so many things you could do. When I was your age I was never bored."

"Oh, well, things were different then. People used to sit around in frocks down to their ankles and sew or something."

"Hey! I'm not as old as all that," replied Aunt Janet, laughing, "and things weren't so different when I was your age. There were always masses of things to do."

"Such as what?"

"Well, I remember on rainy days I used to make leaf-pictures with lard and a candle and things."

"There aren't any leaves on the trees now," said Susan.

"And we don't know how to make leaf-pictures," added Mandy.

"There are always leaves on evergreen trees," replied Aunt Janet, "and I learned to make leaf-pictures at Guides."

"Oh, Guides!" said Susan.

"We've never wanted to be Girl Guides, have we, Mandy?"

"No," said Mandy, "or Brownies."

"You've missed a lot," stated Aunt Janet. "I loved Brownies and Guides. Now listen! We'll go for a picnic this afternoon."

"A picnic in this weather!"

"No, I'm not mad!" laughed Aunt Janet. "I'm just calling on my Guiding skills." She hurried into the kitchen, and the two girls, curious, followed her.

Aunt Janet began packing parcels in a holdall.

"Shall I lay the table?" asked Susan.

"No, thank you."

"Shall I start on the picnic sandwiches?" asked her sister.

"No, thank you. We're not having dinner at home. We're taking it out as a picnic, and we don't need sandwiches. Go and get your coats on."

Mandy and Susan ran upstairs, greatly puzzled.

"D'you suppose we're just taking lettuce, tomatoes and cheese, like we do sometimes in the summer, and eating it with bread-and-butter, unsandwiched?" asked Mandy. "It'll be jolly cold."

"Well, I thought that at first," replied her sister, "but those things she was putting into the holdall didn't look like picnic stuff—in fact—oh, no!—don't say we're going to Granny's!"

"That means we'll have a picnic in the garden, where it's sheltered. I thought it funny that we should be eating out in this weather. Oh, gosh, I don't fancy that!"

"Look," said Susan, "I know it's disappointing for us, but don't let Aunt Janet know. I expect she thought it would be a nice surprise for us. She knows we like going to Granny's, as a rule. Remember what Miss Sanderson said at Sunday School— that grown-ups have feelings the same as children."

"We'll just have to keep smiling and pretend we're thrilled to bits, then," said Mandy gloomily.

They went downstairs and entered the kitchen just in time to see their aunt struggling to get an unusually shaped object, wrapped in greaseproof paper, into the holdall.

"Whatever's that?"

"Is it your tennis-racket?"

"Why are you putting it in greaseproof paper?"

"Never mind," said Aunt Janet. "Come along now. I'm looking forward to our picnic."

They fetched their bicycles and set off. It was quite pleasant riding along. There was no wind and there was still a little frost left from morning, making the hedgerows sparkle. They rode along at a good pace and were soon warm and glowing, especially when they reached the crossroads at the top of the hill near their grandmother's house. Aunt Janet was riding a little way in front of the girls, going over the brow of the hill. The girls, thinking they were going to Granny's, turned left. Mandy's front wheel just caught Aunt Janet's back mudguard. Susan's pedal caught in Mandy's back wheel, and they all fell off and landed in a heap in the road. Luckily, there was very little

Mandy's front wheel caught Aunt Janet's back mudguard

35

traffic about, but none of them was very pleased.

"What the dickens are you up to?" said Aunt Janet, after she had picked herself up and made sure neither of them was hurt.

"Well, it was your fault. You shouldn't have taken such a wide corner," said Mandy, rather rudely, because she was a bit shaken.

"Corner? Who was taking a corner? If I had been turning a corner I'd have put my hand out," Aunt Janet stated.

"Well, I thought you didn't bother because we all knew where we were going."

"You evidently didn't know."

"Well, that's the way to where Granny lives, isn't it?"

"Who said anything about Granny's? It seems we don't all know where we're going. We are going, if you must know, to Willow Woods. Now, are you sure neither of you is hurt? Oh, your belt's broken, Susan. Hang on a minute." Aunt Janet fished in her pocket and took out a safety-pin, with which she fixed the broken belt.

It was a constant source of wonder to the girls that their aunt always seemed able to come up with something useful in an emergency. She always carried safety-pins, clean hankies for grazed knees, pieces of string, which had more than once saved a situation, as at the time one strap of Susan's bicycle basket broke and the other looked in danger of following suit owing to the added strain. Aunt Janet certainly was a handy person to have around. She had told them that it was due to her training in Guides, but they hardly believed her.

"Come along now," she said, "or we'll never get there. You

Aunt Janet fixed the broken belt

should always make signals, even when you feel sure whoever is behind knows where you're going."

They rode on through the bare countryside. Aunt Janet pointed out lots of interesting things that the girls would never have noticed by themselves, and eventually they came to Willow Woods.

"Now to eat," said Mandy, getting off her bike and leaning it against a tree. "What is there for lunch?"

"Not so fast," said Aunt Janet, getting out a penknife, another item she seemed never to be without. It was a handy one with

lots of gadgets in it. "First things first."

Kneeling down, she cut out a large piece of grass about sixty centimetres square, then cut it across diagonally, sliced out the four triangular turves thus made, rolled them up, and put them carefully to one side.

"She's gone haywire," said Mandy, in mock dismay.

"Utterly crazy," said Susan, clasping her sister round the neck and pretending to be terrified.

Ignoring their teasing, which she enjoyed, Aunt Janet said, "Go and collect as many dry, dead holly-leaves as you can from under that bush and bring them back here."

The girls ran off happily. This picnic was different, if nothing else, and they were beginning to enjoy themselves. They collected the leaves. When they returned, they found that their aunt had gathered masses of twigs and sticks and arranged them in different sizes near the bare patch of earth.

"Right! Now we're away," she said, putting the "punk", as she called the twigs and leaves, in the middle of the bare patch. She built up a "wigwam" round the

punk with the wood in ascending order of size. Soon it was all arranged to her satisfaction. Putting a match to it she soon had a fire blazing.

"I can still do it with one match, too," she said, proudly.

"Oh, please may we try?" asked Susan.

"Afterwards," replied Aunt Janet.

"What a good idea to have a fire to sit by," said Mandy. "Shall I get out the food now?"

"Yes, please. You two unpack while I look for some old bits of brick or something". With that, Aunt Janet hurried off into the woods.

"Look at this!" cried Susan suddenly.

Mandy looked and saw that her sister was holding up the parcel they had thought was a tennis-racket. It was a frying-pan!

"Well, I'm bothered!" she exclaimed. "I suppose the other parcels contain bacon and eggs. I hope the eggs didn't get smashed when we fell off our bikes. Let's have a look."

They delved into the bag once more, but could find no bacon or eggs. Instead, they found a large tin of beans, an onion, and some raw minced beef. Their faces fell. Aunty must have brought the shopping by mistake!

Just then their aunt came back, carrying four half-bricks.

"It's amazing what you can find even in a pretty wood, if you just root round for a bit."

She arranged the bricks at each corner of the fire. Then she put the frying-pan on top. The solid dripping in it began sizzling away merrily.

"Now, pass me the mince," she said; then, catching sight of the girls' faces. "Whatever is the matter?"

"We thought you had brought the wrong parcels. Are you really going to cook dinner out here?"

"Of course! A meal like this is easy to an ex-Guide."

The girls were silent and thoughtful as they watched their aunt cook a delicious meal. So this was Guiding! They'd had no notion that it included exciting adventures like this. Even peeling vegetables and cleaning out the frying-pan after wouldn't seem quite such a boring task

"A meal like this is easy to an ex-Guide," declared Aunt Janet

37

as it did at home.

"This is fun!" cried Mandy.

"Well, I think so," said Aunt Janet. "Now you've got the idea you can go off by yourselves sometimes, but make sure the fire is out when you've finished and replace the turves properly. We'll take this old bean-can and other rubbish home."

"I'd like to go camping!" cried Mandy.

"Me, too," said Susan.

"If you joined Guides you'd be able to go camping every year. You'd learn all sorts of useful things too."

"I thought Guides just dressed up in uniform and did good turns," said Susan.

"Well, there's nothing wrong in that," said Aunt Janet, "but I do see your point."

After the meal, which really was excellent and tasted even more so in the open air, Mandy and Susan both practised firelighting, and before the end of the afternoon they could both do it with two matches and Mandy had managed to do it once with only one.

"It may sound ridiculous," said Aunt Janet, "and it will probably never happen, but if ever you do get lost anywhere and happen to find a solitary match in your pocket you may be glad you learned this. It's always well to Be Prepared, as the Guide motto says."

On the way home, Mandy said, "I really will join the Guides."

"So will I," said Susan.

Every Wednesday now, the girls go to their respective meetings. Aunt Janet leaves the house with them. She has become a Guider!

As Mandy and Susan tell their friends, it all came as a result of the surprise picnic.

Toadstool Crossword

by Jean B. Hopkins

Here's a special Brownie crossword puzzle. Your *Brownie Guide Handbook* will help you to find some of the answers if you get stuck. The number of letters in each answer is shown at the end of each clue.

Clues Across

5—Pack Ventures can be indoors or (3,2,5)
7—As good . . gold (2)
8—Another name for myself (2)
9—A play without words (perhaps for the Jester badge) (4)
12—Tommy's sister (5)
13—As number 7 (2)
17—What is a G.C.U.? (it's in the *Handbook*) (4,7,5)
18—To polish your shoes you . . . a duster (3)
20,22—Brownies are W . . . A . . . . (4,5)
21—Who lived in the woods? (4,3)

Clues Down

1—What were Brownies first called? (8)
2—Short for Saint (2)
3—A Noah's Ark is shown on this badge (8)
4—You could take a baby for a walk in this (4)
6—Of whom does a Brownie remember to think? (2,6)
7—The middle letters of CAMP (2)
10—The first and last letters of IMPS (2)
11—Are you enjoying being this? (7)
14—Members of a Brownie Six (4)
15—You can join when you are ten (6)
16—As a Brownie you always do this (3)
19—"Twist me and turn me and show me the . . ." (3)
21—The fourth and seventh letters of Brownie (2)

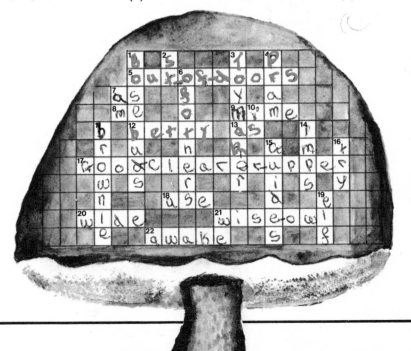

Thinking Day Song

Composed by Brownies of the 1st Wilbrahams Pack, Cambridgeshire, and sung to the tune of "Here we go round the mulberry-bush": contributed by Mrs P. M. Stevens

Chorus:

Here we go round the wide, wide world, the wide, wide world, the wide, wide world;

Here we go round the wide, wide world on our Thinking Day celebration.

Portsmouth Brownies perform a Maori stick game on Thinking Day

Photo: Miss W. J. Beer

Verse 1:

This is the way we wind the wool, wind the wool, wind the wool;
This is the way we wind the wool that comes from the sheep of New Zealand.

Verse 2:

This is the way the sails go round, the sails go round, the sails go round;
This is the way the sails go round on the pretty windmills of Holland.

Verse 3:

This is the way we eat our spaghetti, eat our spaghetti, eat our spaghetti;
This is the way we eat our spaghetti that comes from Italy.

Verse 4:

This is the way we make a street painting, make a street painting, make a street painting;
This is the way we make a street painting in Paris, the capital of France.

Verse 5:

This is the way we milk the cows, milk the cows, milk the cows;
This is the way we milk the cows in Britain's countryside.

Verse 6:

This is the way we tread the grapes, tread the grapes, tread the grapes;
This is the way we tread the grapes in sunny Portugal.

Verse 7:

This is the way we make the toys, make the toys, make the toys;
This is the way we make the toys in factories in Hong Kong.

Suitable actions are done to the words

Australian Brownie Gu

Photo: Weekly Times, Melbourne

South Brownies made a picture-gallery of drawings showing Brownies working on the Eight Points. Their actual drawings, beautifully coloured, are in the book.

Brownies of the 3rd Springvale North and 2nd Balwyn Packs acted as models for photographs, which later helped the artists to make their drawings.

The _Australian Brownie Guide Book_ is written like a story-book and tells how Anne and Sandra join a Brownie Guide Pack. Their Guiders have Aboriginal names—Bookoola, which means Owl, and Kinka, which means Night Owl.

Australian Brownies now have their own special handbook. It is called the _Australian Brownie Guide Book_. In one of the photographs on these two pages you can see three Brownies of the 1st Blackburn South Pack (Victoria) looking at a copy of the book, which their Guider, Mrs Jean Haley, wrote.

Many other Brownies also helped the author and the artists, Mrs Sadie Pascoe and her daughter Suzanne. Several Blackburn

Jennifer Grouse of the 2nd Balwyn Pack looks in the pool, as Betty did in the "Story of the Brownies"

es Lend a Hand

Jean Haley Tells You How

Brownies of the 1st Blackburn Pack carry out "Brownies Keep Fit" by balancing

they find there are little rhymes to help them remember the Eight Points. The rhyme for Brownies Keep Fit is

Now that you're a Brownie,
you're learning how to care
For nails and teeth and skin,
but don't forget your hair.

On the Highway, Australian Brownies can also Lend a Hand by knowing the rules for safety on the beach and in the bush. Every time that Brownies are given a safety rule, a little fairy creature called "Safety Sue" holds up a sign that says either "Stop" or "Think".

The book ends with a Christmas puppet play. Brownies of the 1st Blackburn South had fun making stick-puppets and acting the play.

In the book there is a chapter on conservation where Brownies go on a mystery outing to learn how to take care of nature. They find out many interesting facts at the beach, in the gardens, and in the bush; the "bush" in Australia is wild country.

On their special Thinking Day, Anne and Sandra's Pack travel on a magic carpet and visit Switzerland, South Africa and Mexico, and then they travel back in time to find out how Brownies began.

Australian Brownies have Sixes with Aboriginal names. Anne joins the Moora Moora Six and Sandra joins the Junjarins. When Anne and Sandra begin their first journey, the Footpath,

Brownies of the 3rd Springvale North Pack set out on a mystery outing

Photographs by Suzanne Pascoe

Operation Mountain-top

A GUIDE ADVENTURE STORY IN PICTURES by Rikki Taylor

THE NARROW TRACK ALONG THE QUARRY FACE THAT KIM HAD FOLLOWED PETERED OUT, AND THE BIG PUPPY COULDN'T GO ON OR BACK

45

THE GUIDES REPORTED THEIR DISCOVERY TO THE LOCAL POLICE

AT THE NEXT COMPANY MEETING, THE GUIDER SPOKE ABOUT THE RAVENS' MOUNTAIN-TOP OPERATION

KIM IS NOW THE PATROL MASCOT

THE END

Pack Venture in Jerusalem

by Harriet A. Edmond

Pow-wow came near the end of every meeting of the St. George's Pack of Jerusalem. This was a Pack with a difference. Of the twelve Brownies, six were English, one was Scottish, two were from Canada, one was from Sweden, and two from America. They all lived in Jerusalem because of their fathers' work, and they all loved Brownies, which were run by an English lady they called BeeGee. The Pack were considering a suggestion that for a Pack Venture they should visit all the places associated closely with Jesus.

"The Pixies sure would like to go up the Mount of Olives," said Cindy, American Sixer of the Pixies.

"That's a good idea, Cindy," BeeGee agreed. She noticed that Angela, Sixer of the Gnomes, was signalling to speak. "Yes, Angela?"

"The Gnomes would like to visit the Garden of Gethsemane, BeeGee."

"Well, the Garden is at the foot of the Mount, so both Sixes should get their wish," replied BeeGee. "Would you all like to go next Saturday instead of having our regular meeting here?"

"Yes!" cried the Pack all together, and so it was agreed.

The following Saturday the Brownies piled into BeeGee's little touring bus. Two Ranger Guides, Judith and Carmela, had

come to assist the Brownie Guider.

"We're going to the Church of All Nations, then BeeGee will drive up to the hotel at the top, leave the bus there, come down and join us in the Garden of Gethsemane," Carmela told them.

At the Church of All Nations Bee-Gee clapped her hands to claim the attention of the Brownies.

"Gnomes, I want you to stay with Judith while Carmela looks after the Pixies," she said. "I trust you to do exactly as they say until I get back. It will take me about half an hour to drive around to the top and then come down on foot. By then you should have seen the Church of All Nations and be in the Garden. I'll meet you there."

The Brownies split into their two Sixes.

"Carmela, why is this church called the Church of All Nations?" asked Trudy as they walked towards the side entrance.

"You'll see when we get inside," the Ranger answered, taking Trudy by the hand.

The inside of the church was very dark, and it took the girls several minutes before their eyes grew accustomed to the dimness, and even then a few missed a step down and almost fell.

The other Brownies gathered round as Carmela explained that

sixteen nations had helped in the building of the church. "The coats-of-arms of each of the nation are set into the ceiling above us," she said, "but it's difficult to see them today."

"It would be real nice if they had some light," Cindy said.

"It would spoil the effect, though," Judith said. "When the sun comes round to this side of the valley it brightens the place up, but the bluish-purple window-glass always cuts down the light." She looked round at the Brownies. "See that rock that makes the wall behind the altar? That's where Jesus prayed the night before he was betrayed."

Trudy and the others moved quietly across the mosaic floor, touching the rock and gazing round, particularly at the alabaster windows, until Carmela and Judith called for them to leave.

"We'll go into the Garden now. Gnomes, this is your Venture wish, so you go through first with Judith."

Carmela held the Pixies back as they made to run ahead.

The Garden of Gethsemane was like another world after the shadowy gloom of the church. The sun shone through the olive-trees. As the girls walked along the flagstoned paths, they talked about the size and age of the trees.

Angela, Sixer of the Gnomes, asked, "Is it true that these might be the same trees that were here when Jesus was alive?"

"Yes, it's possible," Judith answered. "It's certain that if they are not they grew from shoots of the trees that were here the night he was betrayed."

"Is this where Judas brought the soldiers?" Trudy asked.

"Yes, this is the spot," answered Carmela.

"The trees are beautiful, aren't they? They're so twisted and bent it's a wonder they grow at all," Judith commented.

BeeGee arrived soon after this, and all the Brownies crowded round to offer her a drink.

"Where are we going now, BeeGee?" Trudy asked as they all prepared to leave the Garden.

"We'll start to climb up the Mount," said the Guider. "We'll have to stay in a single line against the wall and listen for cars. Keep out of the bright sunlight."

The Brownies set off up the hill, finding it hard going after the first few twists in the road.

They visited the Russian Church of St. Mary Magdalene, where they saw a nun who was very, very old. At another stop they saw different types of tombs that people were buried in 2,000 years ago. At the third stop they saw a priest with a long, flowing white beard. The girls enjoyed their climb, but were glad when Bee-Gee led them off into an open space and told them to eat their snacks.

"Isn't the view from here into the old city grand?" said Cindy.

The golden roof of the Dome of the Rock and the silver dome of the Al-aqsa Mosque glittered in the morning sun.

"The road looks as if it should be a river from here," said Trudy.

"It used to be one," said Judith. "The Bible mentions Kidron as a brook, and that's water."

"Eat up, Brownies, then we'll pack up our rubbish and head for the top of the Mount of Olives.

There's a camel sitting up there."

They all started up the hill again, turning only when Cindy pointed out how the sun was catching the gold of the seven onion-shaped spires of the Russian church.

"There's the camel!" Lynn, the Pixie Second, called out, and they all raced along the walled top of the mountain. The camel was sitting contentedly chewing some hay.

"*Shalom, shalom,*" said the camel-keeper as the girls stopped out of reach of the camel's long neck. "You wish to ride?" he asked.

"No, not today," BeeGee replied; "but the girls would like to pet the camel and perhaps have a picture taken."

"For you, lady, I make special

The Dome of the Rock, a shrine of the Arab religion of Islam in Jerusalem

The Mount of Olives, often ascended by Jesus and his disciples

Photographs by Alan Band Associates

▼

Ancient olive-trees in the Garden of Gethsemane, where Jesus was betrayed by Judas

A Jerusalem camel-keeper

gift of picture." The camel-keeper bowed towards the Brownies, and held out his hand to Trudy. "Come, little girl in brown; the camel will not hurt you."

Trudy edged forward nervously until her hand came in contact with the neck of the big animal. It didn't move, and she took courage and patted it as she would pat her dog at home. The other Brownies crowded round, and Judith was able to take a photograph.

The Brownies thanked the camel-keeper for letting them pet his animal, and then hurried into the hotel for the ice-cream Bee-Gee promised them.

All the Brownies agreed that it was a very nice end to their first and very interesting Pack Venture.

"She went to Spain with her Company last year and camped on the Costa Brava."

PLAYTIME

by Jean Howard

ART FOR ALL

Sixes line up in teams. Each Sixer is blindfolded and led to a chair on which are paper and pencil or crayon.

The Guider or Pack Leader calls out the name of an object to be drawn—a house or a fish or a rabbit, or anything else simple.

When all the Sixers have finished drawing, the name of their Six is put on the back of the drawing and the number 1 on the front top corner.

Every member of each Six has a turn, the Guider calling out a different object each time and marking the name of the Six on each drawing.

Finally, someone (perhaps a visitor) is asked to judge the best drawing of the first object, then of the second object, and so on. On turning the winning drawings over it will be seen which Six is the winner. Two points might be awarded for each winning picture.

This game could be adapted for play out of doors as well as indoors. Materials used could be stones on grass or pebbles on a sandy beach. It might lead to an art or collage competition between Packs or Sixes.

MARCH, SKIP, HOP, RUN!

When the Guider or Pack Leader calls out "Soldiers!" all the Brownies march round the hall.

When she calls out "Sprites!" all skip round.

When she calls out "Rabbits!" all hop round.

When she calls out "Witches!" all run to the centre of the hall or to a named tree if the Pack is out of doors. The Brownies must sit or crouch down as if hiding. The last to sit is "out". The game continues until only one Brownie is left, and she is the winner.

All must march or skip or hop round the edge of the hall and not try to stay near the centre in order to be ready for the call of "Witches!"

Another kind of play by Brownies of the 35th Portsmouth Pack

Photo by Miss W. J. Beer

A collage of Australia made by the 24th Colchester Pack is proudly displayed by two of the Brownies

Colour print by Mrs O. Sheppard

Who likes dolls? The children in the Shaftesbury home to whom these are being given will love them. All the dolls were made by Brownies, parents and friends

Colour print by Mrs E. Whitemore

Collecting wildflowers to press for making bookmarks is one of the activities Scottish Brownies enjoy at Glasgow County's Pack Holiday House

Colour print by Miss Sheila Blackwood

"Roll up and roll a car" is the call of the 6th Preston Park Pack, Brighton West, who are helping to raise funds for the parish church at a fete

Colour print by Mrs R. J. Stockham

FUN INDOORS...

and OUTDOORS

Meet the Pearly King and Queen, who are really Brownies of the 3rd High Barnet Salvation Army Pack enjoying themselves at the National Salvation Army Brownie Revels

Colour print by Mrs V. M. Chester

Celebrating the Diamond Jubilee of their Pack, the 1st Windsor Brownies put on plays with royalty looking on—Brownies dressed as Queen Elizabeth I, Queen Victoria, Prince Albert, Queen Elizabeth II and Prince Philip. In the wings are Tudor dancers

Play Acting

Another play performed is the Greek Brownie Story, with a Brownie narrator and Brownie "birds"

Colour prints by Miss D. Watkins

The Christmas Good Turn of the 12th Aylesbury Pack takes the form of a carol-singing procession, complete with Brownies depicting the Holy Family and with lanterns made by the Pack, and a large box of chocolates for patients in Stoke Mandeville Hospital

Colour print by Mrs J. F. Hayes

53

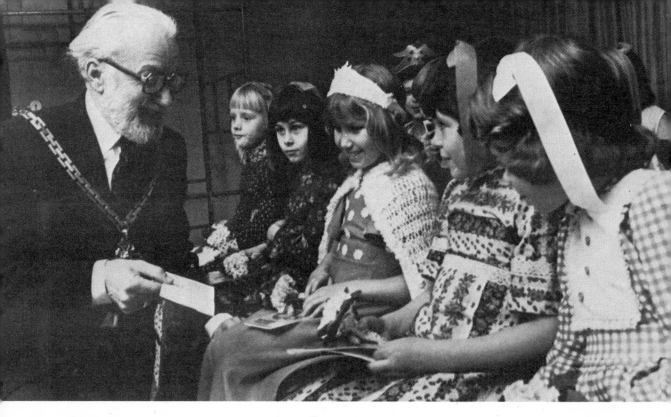

Helping Others

The Mayor of Worcester shows Brownies of the 1st Nunnery Wood Pack at a "Festival of Queens" the cheque they raised for the National Children's Home by collecting five hundred labels, by Pack Ventures, and other activities

Photos by courtesy of Berrow's Newspapers, Worcester

The 57th Nottingham Brownies present a furnished dolls' house to the National Children's Home after raising the money for it by a sponsored walk

Photo by courtesy of Nottingham Evening Post

Brownies to the Rescue

by Daphne M. Pilcher

Fierce storms have swept the forest. Paths are blocked by fallen trees. Streams are flooded. The Brownie Guider in the Brownie House in the heart of the forest has been cut off for days. The Brownies try to take food to her. Which Six manage to get through?

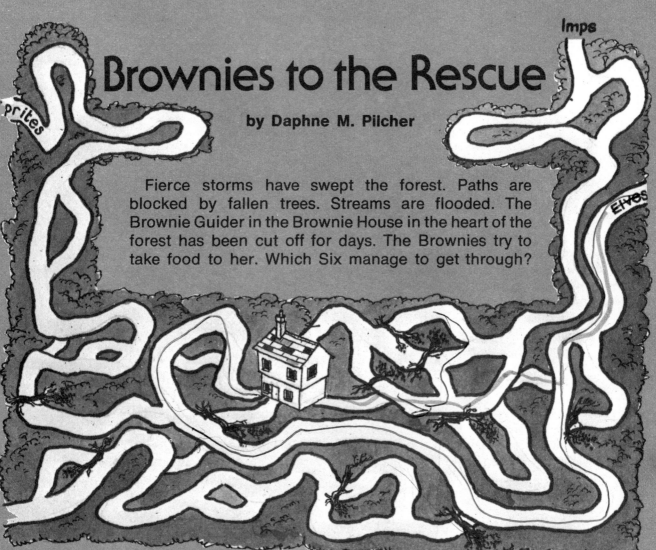

Pair Up the Shapes

by G. R. Siddons

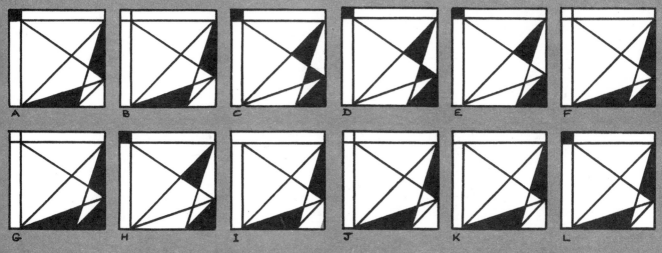

Rachel's Birthday Wish

by Nora Windridge

Rachel had a summer birthday in the long hot month of August. She made a list of all the things that she would like to have. "I'd like a party for my new Brownie friends," she told her mother. "I'd like a bubble bath and a denim dress, but most of all I'd like two guinea-pigs."

Her mother said: "You have a dog and you never take him for walks. You have a cat and you never think of filling her saucer with milk or stroking her. Who would look after the guinea-pigs, do you think?"

Late one hot afternoon Rachel lay drowsing in the garden among the sweet scent of roses and wallflowers. She had put on her Brownie uniform ready for the Pack meeting after tea. Buttercups tickled her nose. By the front gate the dog and the cat sat amiably together. Rachel was half asleep. She saw, or thought she saw, a little man in the hawthorn-hedge. He was only as big as her finger. He wasn't looking at Rachel; he was watching a spider spin a web.

"An elf!" thought Rachel.

She moved a little nearer over the grass. The little man was laughing at the spider spinning its web. Rachel closed her fingers over him and held him high in the air.

The little man laughed no more. "Put me down! Put me down!" he cried.

Rachel said: "I've always wanted a little man like you to keep in my doll's house. You can eat off my little china dishes."

"No, no, no!" cried the little man. "Put me back in the hedge, and I will give you a wish."

"I'd rather have you," said Rachel.

"A wish! A wish!"

"I wish I could understand what my dog and cat are saying," Rachel said, "and I wish I could have . . ."

But as she said "I wish . . ." the little man was out of her hand and into the hedge.

Rachel scowled.

The cat and the dog still lazed in the sun, but now Rachel heard the dog say, "How I would love a long sniffy walk in the sunshine. But Rachel is so lazy; it's not much fun to belong to her."

"Put me down! Put me down!" cried the little man

56

Rachel thought she saw a little man only as big as her finger

The cat said: "At least you have had your dinner. Rachel promised to give me a plate of fish, but she forgot. It's not much fun to belong to Rachel."

"And now she wants guinea-pigs!" said the dog. "Poor things!"

"She will soon get tired of them," agreed the cat. "She will forget their water, forget their cabbage-leaves, forget to put them to play on the grass, forget all about them."

"It's not much fun to belong to Rachel," they both said.

Rachel lay on the grass and listened; she was very pink in the face.

"I wish I hadn't heard what the cat and the dog were saying! It must be horrid to belong to me."

She jumped up and ran into the cool kitchen. "Puss, here's your dinner!" she cried. She

fetched the dog's lead. "Come on, Patch; let's go for a walk!"

She took the dog for his walk every day after that, and the cat never had to wait for her dinner again.

Rachel's mother said, "Rachel is really much more thoughtful these days. I believe she would look after guinea-pigs if we gave them to her for her birthday."

And Rachel does. She remembers their water and their bran and their greenstuff; and she puts them out to play on the grass, in sunshine and shade. She is working for her Animal Lover Badge now. She's glad she heard what the cat and the dog said!

Every day after that she took the dog for his walk

Keeping a Pet Tortoise

by Alan P. Major

A tortoise is one of the easiest creatures to keep as a pet. It is fascinating and interesting—and intelligent, too. It is far from stupid, even if it is slow in movement. It quickly learns to recognise its owner and to hide from strangers. A tortoise has an active, alert mind, and it shares with most children a dislike of rain!

A tortoise is cheap to buy and keep. Prices vary from time to time, but your local pet-shop owner can help you on this point. A young tortoise never costs much to buy. It is a strict vegetarian and loves nothing better than a diet of dandelion leaves and flowers, sow-thistle, and fresh (really *fresh*) lettuce and cabbage leaves. It will also enjoy a piece of soft fruit, such as orange, citrus or apple. Many children who own a tortoise seem to forget that their pet also likes a lot of fresh water and occasionally milk. Give water or milk in a flattish receptacle, so that it can be reached easily. If the tortise has to climb on to it to drink, it may overturn both the drink and itself. Most tortoises tend to get into the habit of climbing, and there is always the risk that it will overturn on to its back. If it does this, unless soon righted, it will die.

A small area of garden with few obstacles in it, but with some shady shrubs (where the leaves and flowers are out of reach) or other form of shade, is ideal. Tortoises do like the sun, but, curiously, they suffer and become tired-out if in the sun for too long a time.

It is not advisable to let them have too free a run in the garden. Many favourite pets meet their "end" by getting lost, straying into strange surroundings or even on to busy roads. But you must give them lots of exercise, especially if they are kept for long periods indoors. If it is possibe, the best means of giving them exercise is to make a moveable pen, from wire and wood, about 46cm (18″) high by 61cm to 91cm (2ft to 3ft) wide and 152cm to 183cm (5ft to 6ft) long. This can be moved around the garden into sunny or shady corners, but alway remember to provide a box or large tin, placed on its side, into which the tortoise can quickly move.

Why the tortoise should dislike rain is unknown and a puzzle. Its carapace (shell), and the horny skin on its head and legs, would amply protect it. It can also swim quite well if it has to, but at the first drops of rain you will see your tortoise make for the nearest shelter as quickly as possible. One I knew would even bury itself in the loose soil of a flower-bed until the rain passed over. It's a wonder it didn't carry an umbrella!

Polish Its Shell

I do not like to see a tortoise's shell painted. Some owners of tortoises paint various colours and even stripes upon the shell. To me this is unnatural and looks horrible. The owners usually claim it helps them to find their pets if they wander in the garden, but there are more sim-

Photo by Alan Band Associates

A tortoise is an odd kind of creature, but friendly and interesting

ple aids than this. Paint a piece of adhesive tape white and stick this upon the top of the shell. It can easily be seen and will peel off it you want to wash or polish the tortoise's shell.

The shell does look much better and smarter when polished. Wash carefully in slightly warm water, keeping it off the body of the tortoise itself, then rub dry. Work in a little oil on the shell and polish with a brush, finally getting a gloss with a soft cloth.

Winter Care

When the first frosty weather arrives do not allow the tortoise to run in the garden pen, but bring it indoors and prepare it hibernating quarters for the winter. Fill a box half full of *dry* soil, straw and wood shavings and place the tortoise on it. Within a short time it will have burrowed in and made itself a warm, cosy nest in which to sleep away the colder winter months. If left in the garden it will bury itself, but a severe

winter might kill it. Even if it survived it might be tempted out by the first early spring sunshine, which might not mean that warm weather had come to stay, although the tortoise might think if had. The first frost, after it had woken up and come out of its burrow in the garden, would kill it. So bring it indoors.

A baby tortoise shouldn't be put into hibernation, but fed and given warm shelter and exercise.

A Hundred Years Old

The most popular type of tortoise kept as a house pet is the Greek or European tortoise (*Testudo graeca*), which comes from the warm eastern Mediterranean regions. When carefully looked after and treated properly it often lives to a great age, passing from generation to generation of owners in the same family. There have been many records of a tortoise living over a hundred years.

If you like a quiet pet, easily and cheaply fed, and one that can be picked up but needs very little care and attention to its body, buy a tortoise. It is a fascinating creature.

At the Revels

Concorde not only catches the eyes of thousands of spectators but makes an excellent shelter when it rains (1)

Birds of a feather flock together at the County Revels at Gloucester, where thousands of Brownies enjoy a thrilling afternoon (2)

Ladies and gentlemen from a hundred years ago add colour and gaiety to the scenes of revelry at Gloucester (3)

Colour slides by Robert Moss

RUM RHYMES

by Aileen E. Passmore

CATHERINE WHEELS

I'd like a bike with Catherine-wheels.
  How everyone would stare
When I went whizzing down the road,
  To see them sparkling there!
I wouldn't need a lamp at all,
  'Cos if I rode at night
The shining, sparkling Catherine-wheels
  Would shed a lovely light!

THE FUNNY HOUSE

I came upon a funny house
   Down in the wood last night.
The roof was made of sugar-loaf,
   With chimneys pink-and-white.
It had a door of chocolate-cream,
   With toffee-apple knob;
A queer man lives inside the house,
   Because I saw him bob
Behind the curtains trimmed with sweets;
   I saw him plain as plain
Just for a second, and tonight
   I'll go and look again!

Can you see the funny man? yes

Grow-Your-Own Challenges

by Anne Phillips

You've probably grown a carrot-top in a saucer and seen it sprout feathery green leaves, and you've almost certainly grown mustard-and-cress on a flannel from seeds. Now try something different. Collect vegetables like swedes, turnips, radishes, beetroot and parsnips. Slice the top or crown from each vegetable and space them out in a big dish. By the way, the term "green fingers" doesn't mean fingers sliced off and grown, so be careful!

Spread a thin layer of sand over the bottom of your dish, then top it up with water every day. Put a bit of coal in to keep the water sweet.

When you go into woods, collect nuts and fruits like acorns, beechnuts, hazel-nuts, conkers, ash-keys and sycamore-seeds. With these you can make your own little forest. Beg an old meat-tin from Mummy and fill it with soil, leaf-mould and moss. Make some hills and hollows with stones so that your forest will look natural. Place the fruits and nuts in the soil, then leave the tray out of doors until the winter frost has frozen it once or twice. Then bring the tray indoors and put it in a sunny window. When grown, you will have a lovely mini-forest.

Thistles will help to make your mini-forest look real

You can grow lots of things in bottles and jars, of all shapes and sizes. Put an acorn or a conker in the top of a bottle or a potato on top of a jar. Fill the jar or bottle with water, which must

only just touch whatever you are growing. You will be surprised at the growth that results. Put a piece of coal in the water.

You could grow a hyacinth

62

bulb like this too. Plant it in the autumn. It will soon grow and throw out long white roots.

Here is another good idea. Paint an egg-tray any colour that you fancy. Do the same with egg-shells. Then fill the shells with soil and plant with seeds like virginia-stock or sweet-smelling mignonette. April or May is a good time for planting. The seeds will take about eight weeks to grow. Put the egg-shells into the compart-ments of the tray to give them support.

Try growing fruit-pips. Collect pips from an orange, a lemon or a grapefruit. Put each pip into a separate plant-pot containing ordinary soil, and before long you will have some tiny fruit-trees. Some pips take longer than others, so do not be too anxious for results. You will be very lucky if you get any fruit, though!

To tell which tree is which if you forget to label them, rub your fingers gently on the leaves, and you will soon know from the smell what it is. If you put your pips into a dish all together you will create a small orchard.

Do you happen to have an orange-tree in your house? If so, take one of the berries from it and let it dry out. Then break it open and plant the seeds that are inside. One may develop into a lovely orange-tree.

Jigsaw Puzzle Picture

To find out what this puzzle picture is, copy the drawing in each square on the left into the square on the right with the same number. Then you will have a complete picture.

Oliver the Otter finds a log a useful landing-place

Brock the Badger roots about for his supper

Night-shift in the Countryside

by Daphne M. Pilcher

When we go to bed we expect everything and everyone else to be doing the same, but this does not happen. It is certainly much more difficult to see what is going on around us at night, but out in the countryside there is a great deal of activity.

As dusk falls the first of the night-shift begin to appear. The badger ambles from its sett just after sunset. It is difficult to know why some animals feed at night. For instance, today, the badger's only enemy is man (who should not be), so he could probably manage to feed by day, but in the dim and distant past there was probably a very good reason for him to keep out of sight during the daylight hours.

The fox, who is the only wild relative of the dog to be found in Britain, does his hunting at night. He is as stealthy as a cat and will eat frogs, hedgehogs, squirrels, voles, mice, rats and rabbits. He will also scavenge from dustbins in built-up areas. Both badger and fox find the hedgehog a tasty meal. The fox draws the line at eating the skin, but the badger devours it all.

Some animals are not active all night long but do their feed-ing at dusk and again at dawn. The rabbit and the deer are both dusk and dawn feeders. Hares feed mainly at twilight on grass, roots, bark, and the produce of field and garden. We call these creatures who are active at night nocturnal.

As darkness falls, the bat takes to the air to hunt for food. He has poor eyesight, but has a kind of built-in radar that enables him to find food—mainly insects—and also to avoid running into obstacles.

The hedgehog roams around at night seeking slugs, worms, and sometimes an adder, who will be on the move if the night is warm. The hedgehog is immune to the adder's poison. The hedgehog has a keen sense of smell and hearing, which equip him well for night work.

The dormouse, who looks more like a small squirrel than a mouse—he has a bushy tail hunts for insects, berries, seeds and leaves by night, but, like the shrew, he makes a tasty meal for the owl. The shrew is a noisy, quarrelsome and restless insect-eating mammal who is active both day and night.

The rat is a shy, nocturnal

Osbert Owl makes sure of his next meal

65

animal. The brown rat is a very good swimmer.

The solitary, secretive otter is rarely seen today. He lies up by day on a river-bank in reeds or in his home (called a holt). At night, when he wanders, he keeps to a regular beat, working up and down a river and often travelling great distances overland. His favourite foods are eels, salmon, and trout.

Owls are well known for their night activities, but another bird who becomes active as darkness falls is the nightjar. He is a visitor from Africa and arrives in May. He spends his day on the ground well camouflaged by his mottled-brown plumage, which makes it difficult to distinguish him from dead leaves or wood. He is an inquisitive bird. His main source of food is large moths.

Most moths are around only at night. Perhaps they feel safer, since there are considerably more birds around in the day than there are at night. They are well equipped for the night-shift too. Their feathery antennae are very sensitive to smells, and even at night they'll find the scented flowers. Their wing patterns and colouring camouflage them marvellously when they are resting during the day against tree-trunks, lichen-covered rocks, etc.

Hidden under moss and dead leaves during the day, the rounded snail emerges at night to feed on fungi and decaying matter.

One of the most interesting night sights in the country is the steady blue-green glow on decaying tree-trunks that is a sign that honey fungus is growing there. This was once actually used to light the way along dark paths. The wingless female glow-worm produces a light that is used to attract her flying mate.

If you go out in the country at dusk do keep your eyes open. Don't forget the night-shift will be at work!

Reynard the Fox peeps from the undergrowth ready for a night's hunt

Whatever's Happened to Me?

When Mummy called me a lazy child
I very impolitely smiled,
And turned my back on washing-up
So I could read my favourite book.

When Mummy called me a naughty girl
I'd flounce away with skirts a-twirl,
And do the exact opposite to
The things she said I had to do.

Well, isn't it funny how things have changed?
My room I've tidily re-arranged;
I'm running errands—and what is more
I'm even doing jobs next door!

I wonder if you can possibly guess
The reason for all my helpfulness?
I'm sure you could if you really tried—
I've just become a Brownie Guide!

—M.M.A

Caroline Joins the Sprites

by Doris Bellringer

Caroline was thrilled at the idea of wearing a uniform. Last Christmas her aunt had given her a nurse's outfit and before that she had worn a cowboy suit, but everyone knew that these were only play-clothes. She hadn't been a real nurse or a real cowboy. Now she was going to be a real Brownie and wear a real uniform.

Next Monday was to be her first meeting, and the week seemed endless, but at last Monday arrived and Caroline went with her mother to the church hall where the Brownies met. Caroline wasn't really prepared for the noise and excitement that greeted her. She felt very small in her pink dress. The other girls in their lovely brown uniforms with yellow ties and shining Promise badges all seemed to be bigger than she was. They all seemed to be friends too, but Caroline didn't know anyone.

The Brownie Guider called to Caroline, and then to one of the biggest girls. "Here you are, Caroline, this is your Sixer, Fiona; she'll look after you."

The Sixer took Caroline's hand and ran with her to a small group in the far corner. Mum was having a long conversation with the Brownie Guider, and Caroline felt very lonely. She also felt that she didn't really belong—not in her pink dress.

The Sixer introduced her to all the girls in the Six and told her, "You're going to be a Sprite, and this is our Six emblem." She

Fiona took Caroline's hand and ran with her

pointed to the little green man emblem on her uniform. "You'll have one when you make your Promise."

Caroline nodded. She hoped she wasn't going to cry, but her eyes were beginning to feel a bit damp. Just then the Brownie Guider called her.

"There are lots of things for you to learn before you can be a proper Brownie," she said, "but your Mummy has got the *Brownie Guide Handbook*, and you will learn a lot about Brownies from that."

When she reached home, Mummy read from the *Brownie Guide Handbook* and explained what had to be done before Caroline received her Promise badge.

"The Brownie Guider told me how much the uniform costs," said Mummy. "It's a lot of money for me to find, but the Guider says you can't make your Promise for at least four weeks, so perhaps I'll have time to save up for it." Caroline's mummy was a widow and had a job to make ends meet.

Caroline couldn't sleep that night. She wanted to be a proper Brownie, but the meeting had been rather confusing. All the other girls seemed to know exactly what to do all the time, and some had funny names like Sixer and Second. Caroline loved their smart brown uniform and longed for one herself. "Mummy must manage it!" she whispered to herself as she fell asleep.

She was up early next morning, for she wanted to tell her best friend at school all about Brownies. Mary was too young to join. She was only six and three-quarters.

"There's a Sixer and a Sec-

"You're going to be a Sprite"

ond," Caroline told Mary, "and we have a Brownie Ring."

"A ring? What's that?" asked Mary.

"We dance round and sing a song, and I've got to learn the words before next week. I'm going to have a uniform for when I make my Promise—" she hesitated—"if Mummy can manage to afford it."

At playtime Caroline was showing Mary and Anne one of the games she had played the previous evening when one of the big girls, who was in the top class, came across to her and said, "Hello, Caroline! You came to our Brownies last night."

"Yes," answered Caroline. "I'm going to join."

"I know! You're going to be a Sprite. I'm the Elf Sixer."

Mary and Anne had moved away when the big girl came up, and Caroline felt rather shy.

"Cheerio! See you next week." The Elf Sixer ran back to her friends.

"That was one of our Brownies," Caroline explained to Mary and Anne. "She's the Elf Sixer and I'm a Sprite. I've got a Sixer too. She's got a lot of badges on her arm."

Every night that week Caroline worried her mother about the uniform until Mummy began to get cross. "I've said I'll see about it," she said, "but if you keep pestering me you won't help, so please wait patiently for four weeks."

The Brownie Guider had said she must wait, so Caroline would have to wait. She learnt her Promise and the Law during the four weeks that followed and found out all about the Brownie Ring and the Salute. She began to feel almost as if she was now a real Brownie, but she still wore her pink dress.

Then the awful thing hap-

Mummy began to get cross

Caroline stood speechless. Then she rushed downstairs.

"Thank you! Oh, thank you, Mummy! You did manage it, after all!"

"I'm afraid I didn't," said Mummy, "but Grandma did. It's a present to you from Grandma and Grandpa."

Caroline flung her arms round Grandma's neck and hugged and kissed her. Then she rushed upstairs to get changed. She was going to be a real Brownie in a real Brownie uniform!

pened. "I'm afraid I shan't be able to afford a uniform for you by next week," Mummy told Caroline. "The Brownie Guider said that needn't stop you from making your Promise. You can be a very good Brownie without a uniform, I will see if I can get you a secondhand one soon."

Caroline didn't want to be a Brownie without a uniform, and she wasn't sure that she wanted a secondhand one either, but she didn't say this to the Brownie Guider.

The great day arrived when Caroline was to make her Promise. Grandma was coming to tea so that she could come with Mummy and watch the ceremony. Caroline didn't hurry home from school. She longed to be a Brownie, but she didn't feel right wearing her ordinary pink dress.

She kissed Grandma and then went up to her bedroom. She didn't want Grandma to see how miserable she was. She opened the door. Then she stopped and stared. There, on the bed, all spread out, was a new Brownie uniform, a yellow tie, and a belt.

Caroline flung her arms round Grandma and hugged her

Which Animals in the Ark?

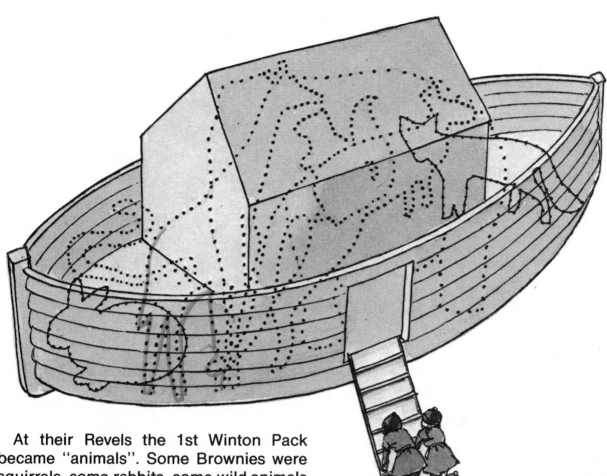

At their Revels the 1st Winton Pack became "animals". Some Brownies were squirrels, some rabbits, some wild animals like giraffes and buffalo. But the rain came down in torrents. Tawny found a shelter and called it the Ark. The Brownie "animals" went into it, singing:—

The animals went in one by one, hurrah, hurrah!
The animals went in two by two, hurrah, hurrah!
The animals went in three by three, the Sixers and the Seconds too
And they all stayed dry in the Ark until the morning.

Can you tell by the shapes which animals went into the Ark?

Time for Play

"Squeak, Little Piggy, Squeak!"

At the 2nd New Thundersley Pack's Summer Recess Party

Time to Eat

For the 2nd New Thundersley Pack, Essex

◄ **A long drink for Jackie Frewin**

Photos by Michael Frewin

A joke and a laugh for Catherine Everett and Julie Howes

72

◄ **Another kind of play by Brownies of the 35th Portsmouth Pack**
Photo by Miss W. J. Beer

"Mind our legs!"
Photos by Melvyn Frewin

◄ **A good feed for Susan Pepper**

A tasty snack for Mandy Dyer

HOW TO MAKE

Egg~cup Sets

Fun With Eggs
by Lena Baker

You can make attractive egg-cup sets out of bonded poly-styrene egg-boxes.

Materials required: Empty polystyrene egg-boxes, prefer-ably the type that come in pretty colours, although the plain cardboard sort will do; scissors; tape-measure or ruler; pencil; contact glue; a small tin of enamel paint if the plain type of egg-box is used.

How to make: Carefully mea-sure and mark around the little containers that the eggs rest in. Carefully cut along the marks. You should get six shapes out of one box. As you need two pieces for each egg-cup, it is possible to get half a dozen pretty egg-cups out of two egg-boxes holding half a dozen eggs.

Stand one shape down, the widest part to the table. Apply a little contact glue to the bottom. At the same time put a little to the same end of another shape. Allow both to dry slightly, then place firmly together. Leave to dry. Contact glue bonds this type of polystyrene together very successfully.

If you have used the plain type of cardboard egg-containers, when you have joined them together give them a coat of enamel paint and let it dry.

These egg-cups are very pretty, lightweight and service-able. The cup part is a perfect container for an egg. You might sell them for your Pack funds.

Egg Mice

Next time you have friends to tea try giving them egg-mice with salad. They will vote it an excellent meal.

You need one hard-boiled egg for each guest, a little tomato sauce and some odds and ends from your salad.

What You Do. Shell your egg and place it down lengthwise; to make it stand cut a sliver from the bottom. The narrow pointed end becomes the head of your mouse.

Take a stem of watercress. Plucking off the green leaf, insert this into the egg as a tail.

Take two shorter lengths, cut-ting the leaf to an ear-like shape. Insert these into the head on each side to form ears. You could use potato-crisps for ears if you prefer.

Two spots of tomato sauce give your mouse pink eyes. For whiskers cut two watercress stalks down the centre and insert them into the sides of the egg.

All you have to do now is to arrange your mouse on a plate of green salad. Does it look almost too good to eat?

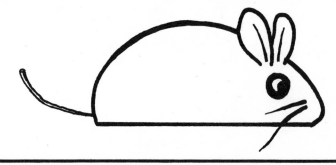

WHICH BADGE?

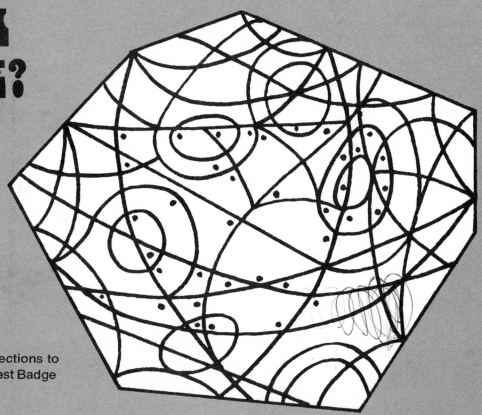

Shade in the dotted sections to find a clue to the Interest Badge

WHICH WAY?

Can you find your way to the house on top of the hill, after going through the stile?

75

Win a New Bike and £50 in This Easy Competition

All you have to do is to put the six delightful pictures on pages 78 and 79 in the order in which you like them. For example, if you like **F** best you put **F** as number 1, the letter of your next choice as number 2, and so on down to number 6. Whatever your age you have as much chance as anyone else of winning the wonderful prize of a new bike for yourself and £50 for your Pack.

The Editor has made his choice. If your first choice agrees with his, you will gain three points; if your second agrees with his, you will gain two points; for each of the others that agrees, one point will be awarded. The competitor with the most points will win the grand double prize. Something of equal value to the bike can be chosen, if preferred.

Fill in the entry form, then on a separate sheet of paper write down in not more than fifty words what you like most about being a Brownie. Take care with this write-up, because it will be taken into account if there are competitors with the same number of points.

Attach your write-up to the entry form and post it to "PICK THE PICTURES" PRIZE COMPETITION, PURNELL BOOKS, BERKSHIRE HOUSE, QUEEN STREET, MAIDENHEAD, SL6 1NF, to arrive not later than March 31, 1980. The winner will be notified as soon as possible after this date.

"PICK THE PICTURES" COMPETITION ENTRY FORM

Just put the picture's letter in the order of your choice

1 ....
2 ....
3 ....
4 ....
5 ....
6 ....

My name is ....
My address is ....
....
....
....**My age is**...........
My Pack is ....
My Guider's name and address is ....
....

Don't forget to write up why you like being a Brownie

Answers to Puzzles and Quizzes

FIND THE OWL (p. 12): Elf.
DIAL A LETTER (p. 13): Missing letter is D; letters spell **GIRL GUIDES. SQUIRREL PUZZLE** (p. 13): Toad, Hare, Mole, Seal, Stoat, Mouse, Rabbit, Squirrel

BROWNIES TO THE RESCUE (p. 55): The Elves

20 QUESTIONS (p. 5): 1—February 22nd, which was the joint birthday of the late Lord and Lady Baden-Powell; 2—Pathfinder; 3—Stop, look, listen; 4—north-east; 5—the three parts of the Promise; 6—blue and white; 7—a get-together of a number of Packs; 8—at ten or over; 9—boil (bubble); 10—Kelpies, Imps, Leprechauns, Ghillie Dhus, Bwbachods; 11—Tommy and Betty; 12—April 23rd;

13—arms horizontal to the ground (pointing left and right), dot-dash-dot; 14—shut and fasten them; 15—November 30th; 16—March 1st; 17—Netherlands (Holland); 18—Rosebuds; 19—reef-knot; 20—Just above your Six Emblem

WITCH PUZZLE (p. 19): Clothespeg

WHICH BADGE? (p. 75): Hostess

PAIR UP THE SHAPES (p. 55): A and L, B and J, C and D, E and H, F and G, I and K

TRICKY TEASERS (p. 30): 16 cubes; clowns' flowers are different; crossword: 1—weasel, 2—squirrel, 3—mouse, 4—badger, 5—vole

TOADSTOOL CROSSWORD (p. 38): *Across:* 5-out of doors; 7-as; 8-me; 9-mime; 12-Betty; 13-as; 17-Good Clearer Upper; 18-use; 20, 22-Wide Awake; 21-wise owl. *Down:* 1-Rosebuds; 2-St; 3-Toymaker; 4-pram; 6-of others; 7-am; 10-is; 11-Brownie; 14-Imps; 15-Guides; 16-try; 19-elf; 21-we

WHICH ANIMALS IN THE ARK? (p. 71): Giraffe, elephant, snake, fox, rabbit, squirrel, kangaroo

GOODNIGHT!

2nd Llanelli Brownies and Guides sing goodnight to the audience at their annual concert—and say goodnight to you too!

Photo: Llanelli Star

77

'Pick the Pictures' Prize Competition

Cocky likes his morning ride

Sammy Seagull sings for his supper

"Hey, stop—I can't swim!"